ك وأنـواعـه

THE MANY S

SHIRK

By

Fadlur Rahman Kalim Kashmiri

Translated & abridged by

Khola Hasan

Foreword by

Dr. Suhaib Hasan

DARUSSALAM
GLOBAL LEADER IN ISLAMIC BOOKS

Riyadh • Jeddah • Sharjah • Lahore
London • Houston • New York

First Edition: December 1996

© **Maktaba Dar-us-Salam, 1996**
King Fahd National Library Cataloging-in-Publication Data
Hasan, Suhaib
The many shades of shirk-Riyadh.
64p., 14x21 cm (understanding Islam series; 3)
ISBN 9960-740-62-5
1-Unbeliever of Allâh I-Title II-Series
219.1 dc. 0104/16
Legal Deposit no. 0104/16
ISBN 9960-740-62-5

Headquarters:

P.O. Box: 22743, Riyadh 11416, KSA
Tel: 00966-1-4033962/4043432
Fax:00966-1- 4021659
E-mail: darussalam@naseej.com.sa
Website: http:// www.dar-us-salam.com
Bookshop: Tel & Fax: 00966-1-4614483

Branches & Agents:

K.S. A.

- Jeddah: Tel: 00966-2-6712299 Fax: 6173448
- Al-Khobar: Tel: 00966-3-8948106

U.A.E.

- Tel: 00971-6-5511293 Fax: 5511294

PAKISTAN

- 50 Lower Mall, Lahore
  Tel: 0092-42-724 0024 Fax: 7354072
- Rahman Market, Ghazni Street
  Urdu Bazar, Lahore
  Tel: 0092-42-7120054 Fax: 7320703

U. S. A.

- Houston: P.O. Box: 79194 Tx 77279
  Tel: 001-713-722 0419 Fax: 001-713-722 0431
  E-mail: Sales @ dar-us-salam.com
  Website: http:// www.dar-us-salam.com
- New York: 572 Atlantic Ave, Brooklyn
  New York-11217
  Tel: 001-718-625 5925

U.K.

- London: Darussalam International Publications Ltd.
  P.O. Box: 21555, London E10 6XQ
  Tel: 044-7947 306 706 Fax: 0044-208 925 6996
- Birmingham: Al-Hidaayah Publishing & Distribution
  436 Coventry Road, Birmingham B10 OUG
  Tel: 0044-121-753 1889 Fax: 121-753 2422

AUSTRALIA

- Lakemba NSW: ICIS: Ground Floor 165-171, Haldon St.
  Tel: (61-2) 9758 4040 Fax: 9758 4030

MALAYSIA

- E&D BOOKS SDN.BHD.-321 B 3rd Floor, Suria Klcc
  Kuala Lumpur City Center 50088
  Tel: 00603-21663433 Fax: 459 72032

SINGAPORE

- Muslim Converts Association of Singapore
  Singapore- 424484
  Tel: 0065-440 6924, 348 8344 Fax: 440 6724

SRI LANKA

- Darul Kitab 6, Nirmal Road, Colombo-4
  Tel: 0094-1-589 038 Fax: 0094-74 722433

KUWAIT

- Islam Presentation Committee
  Enlightment Book Shop
  P.O. Box : 1613, Safat 13017 KUWAIT
  Tel: 00965-244 7526, Fax: 240 0057

BANGLADESH

- 30 Malitola Road, Dhaka-1100
  Tel: 0088-02-9557214, Fax: 0088-02-9559738

Contents

Foreword 5

Chapter 1. Three Forms of Worship.. 9

Chapter 2. Common forms of man-made gods 10

Chapter 3. *Shirk* is a Great Injustice 13
- *Shirk* is an unforgivable sin.
- Heaven has been made *Haraam*.
- All the good deeds of a *Mushrik* are wasted.

Chapter 4. The beliefs of a *Mushrik* Society 15
- *Shirk* in Allâh's person
- *Shirk* in Allâh's attributes
- *Shirk* in Allâh's capabilities
- *Shirk* in Allâh's Rights

Chapter 5. The Portrayal of Allâh in the Qur'an 16

Chapter 6. No Comparison between the Creator and His creation .. 18

Chapter 7. The Beliefs of the Arab non-believers 21

Chapter 8. Everything is in the hands of Allâh.................... 24

Chapter 9. Man and his Needs... 27
- Can a human fulfill our needs.
- The story of Moses in Madyan.

Chapter 10. Prayers for Miracles 32
- The battle of Uhud
- To abandon prayer is *Kufr*.

Chapter 11. The emergence of *Shirk* 36
- Kinship between Allâh and his Creation.
- Allâh's infatuation with His Creation.
- The concept of *Tawassul* (Intercession)

- Allâh Almighty has no need for mediators.
- Ignorance.
- Everything is under the total control of Allâh.
- Mankind is the best creation of Allâh.
- Mankind has no lord or master except Allâh.
- The prophets are the creatures of Allâh.
- Miracles are the work of Allâh Alone.

Chapter 12. Custom and *Shirk* 44
- The elite and *Shirk*.
- The Pharisees.

Chapter 13. Excess and exaggeration 50

Chapter 14. God Incarnate 58
- Hussein Ibn Mansoor Hallaj.
- The concept of *Hulool* is false.
- The death of God.

Chapter 15. Man and God are one?. 61

Chapter 16. Why doesn't Allâh stop *Shirk*? 62
- And fight them until oppression in no more.

FOREWORD

Suppose you have set forth on a long and hazardous journey which takes you to an unpopulated land where even the basic necessities of life are scarce and where your search for food and water is in vain. At the moment of acute despair, a magnificent palace looms up in front of you. A man at its gate beckons you inside and invites you to a delicious meal. Without having to pay a penny you are then offered a room for as long as you like. You would naturally wonder at the identity of the person who has been so generous and hospitable to you. It would be the height of ingratitude not to wish to meet your benefactor and thank him wholeheartedly.

This is, in fact, the story of man and his Creator, Allâh, the Master and Sustainer of the entire universe. We live in the beautiful world that He has created, and we enjoy the innumerable comforts and joys with which He has surrounded us. Is it then not our duty to recognize Him, praise Him and thank Him?

To understand Allâh the Almighty in a manner that suits His Glory and Greatness is *Tawheed* (Oneness of Allâh). To be His obedient servant throughout our lives is only the minimum demonstration of our deep gratitude and debt to Him. Unfortunately, mankind has repeatedly deviated from the path of *Tawheed*, and *Shirk* (associating partners with Allâh) has emerged in many different forms and colours. Allâh has not left His creatures to their own devices, however, but has sent His Prophets, from Adam until Muhammad (صلى الله عليه وسلم), to guide humanity out of the abyss of *Kufr* and *Shirk*. As *Shirk* has always found an opening through the ages, it is essential for us to recognize it in its different guises and to avoid it, because, of all the sins, *Shirk* is the greatest and can never be forgiven.

The author of this booklet, Fadl-ur-Rahman Kalim, has successfully dealt with this subject in a comprehensive yet simple way. The worthy translator, Khola Hasan, has rendered the Urdu text into English, allowing herself the freedom to summarize where necessary, but keeping very close to the original text.

May Allâh guide us all to His straight and true path which leads to Paradise. *Ameen.*

Suhaib Hasan
Chairman
Al-Quran Society.

Publishers Note

The basic concept of Islam is Monotheism. It confirms the belief in Allâh's Oneness without assigning partners to Him in worship. No doubt, the adherents of other religions also hold belief in God but they join partners with Him. For instance, the Jews call Prophet Uzair عليه السلام as son of God. The Christians call Prophet 'Îsâ (Jesus) عليه السلام as son of God. The Hindus split God into many deities. According to their belief, God incarnates in human form to punish the wrongdoers, removes injustice and oppression from the world and fills it with justice, equality and prosperity. In short, all other religions except Islam have a combination of God and His partners or incarnates.

In Islam, *Shirk* (polytheism) is the grievous sin that can not be forgiven until man turns to Allâh in repentance sincerely and asks His pardon .

The present book deals with *Shirk* thoroughly and highlights its various forms in vague among the Muslims and non-Muslims. Its aim is to arouse mass awareness against the *Shirk* and invite them to the Islamic Monotheism based on the Qur'ân and Sunnah. The book, because of its eloquent yet simple and lucid style, gained much popularity. Darussalam has the honour to publish it in the greater interest of the people. Our purpose is to serve Islam and provide the readers with good, knowledgeable and authentic reading material on the subjects related to the Islamic faith.

I expect that the people will get benefited by it and develop their knowledge about polytheism and its consequences; and avoid indulging therein, for it devours their good deeds.

May Allah bless us with the correct religious knowledge and keep us away from perversion appeared in the form of self-designed ideas leading to polytheism and innovations.

Abdul Malik Mujahid
General Manager

IN THE NAME OF ALLÂH,
THE MOST GRACIOUS,
THE MOST MERCIFUL

Chapter 1

THREE FORMS OF WORSHIP

Each religion has some practices and procedures that are called worship. Worship can be oral, physical or monetary.

Oral worship is to pray to someone, appeal to someone when in need, to chant someone's name in reverence, to address someone as the fulfiller of all needs and the helper of all those in distress, to swear an oath in someone's name, to believe that someone has the power to forgive.

Physical worship includes to prostrate or bow down to someone, to direct your life in obedience to someone's command for their pleasure and reward, to print or engrave the name or symbol of someone on your body or possessions in order to be blessed for it.

Monetary worship is to give charity in the name of someone, to harvest some land or rear an animal that has been dedicated to someone; to make a pilgrimage to a place connected with that being in order to worship and rejoice thereby decorating the place, offering sacrifices and gifts, considering the water there to be blessed and the environment to be sacred.

Allâh alone deserves to be worshipped and revered. Islam considers all the above to be legitimate forms of worship, but maintains that Allâh alone should be the object of this worship. Except for Islam, all other religions have made room for the worship of beings others than Allâh. History shows that man-made worship has not been confined to that of statues and pictures of ancestors only but has taken many different forms, some of which will be elucidated in the following pages.

Chapter 2

COMMON FORMS OF MAN-MADE GODS

In his ignorance, man has given many things the status of deities, some of the most famous of which are the following:

1. **Objects of Nature.** Man has worshipped beautiful stones, useful or ferocious animals, the solid trees, towering mountains, flowing streams, volcanoes, even dreadful diseases, the sun, the stars and other planets.
2. **The Noble Prophets.** The disbelieving Arabs used to worship Prophets Ibrahim (Abraham) and Ismail (Ishmail عليهما السلام), the Jews worshipped Prophets Ya'qoub (Jacob) and Uzair (Ezra عليهما السلام), and the Christians worshipped Prophet 'Isa (Jesus عليه السلام).
3. Some have worshipped jinns and demons in their ignorance.

﴿ بَلْ كَانُوا يَعْبُدُونَ الْجِنَّ أَكْثَرُهُم بِهِم مُّؤْمِنُونَ ﴾ [سبأ : ٤١]

"Indeed they worshipped the jinn and many of them had faith in them." (Surah Saba:41)

4. **Kings and Sultans.** In India, China and Japan, emperors and rulers have been worshipped for centuries. Hindus believe that the body of the king is made from heavenly clay and so worshipping it brings divine pleasure.
5. **Angels.** Arab non-believers used to consider angels to be the daughters of God and so made them an object of worship.

﴿ وَيَوْمَ يَحْشُرُهُمْ جَمِيعًا ثُمَّ يَقُولُ لِلْمَلَائِكَةِ أَهَٰؤُلَاءِ إِيَّاكُمْ كَانُوا يَعْبُدُونَ ﴾

[سبأ : ٤٠]

"On that Day He will gather them all and will ask the angels: Are these the people who used to worship you?" (Saba: 40)

6. **Pious Ancestors.** The Prophet (صلى الله عليه وسلم) said: "These people were such that if there was a pious man among them who died, they built a mosque on his grave and made statues of him in it. These people will be the most despised people on the Day of Judgment." Narrated by Bukhari, Muslim, Nasai and Ahmad. The next obvious step was to worship the statues themselves rather than the people they represented.

﴿ ۞ وَإِذْ قَالَ إِبْرَٰهِيمُ لِأَبِيهِ ءَازَرَ أَتَتَّخِذُ أَصْنَامًا ءَالِهَةً إِنِّىٓ أَرَىٰكَ وَقَوْمَكَ فِى ضَلَٰلٍ مُّبِينٍ﴾ [الأنعام: ٧٤]

"And when Ibrahim said to his father Azar — do you take statues as your gods? Indeed I see you and your tribe in clear ignorance." (Surah Al-An'âm:74)

Worshipping the graves of honoured elders is still common today, even among Muslims, despite the punishment that it entails. The Prophet (صلى الله عليه وسلم) said: "Allâh has cursed the Jews and the Christians because they turned the graves of their Prophets into mosques." (Bukhari, Muslim, Ahmad)

Honouring the relics of ancestors and sacrificing to them is prevalent among Hindus, Buddhists and Christians.

﴿ حُرِّمَتْ عَلَيْكُمُ ٱلْمَيْتَةُ وَٱلدَّمُ وَلَحْمُ ٱلْخِنزِيرِ وَمَآ أُهِلَّ لِغَيْرِ ٱللَّهِ بِهِۦ وَٱلْمُنْخَنِقَةُ وَٱلْمَوْقُوذَةُ وَٱلْمُتَرَدِّيَةُ وَٱلنَّطِيحَةُ وَمَآ أَكَلَ ٱلسَّبُعُ إِلَّا مَا ذَكَّيْتُمْ وَمَا ذُبِحَ عَلَى ٱلنُّصُبِ﴾ [المائدة: ٣]

Forbidden to you (for food) are: *Al-Maitah* (the dead animals — cattle — beast not slaughtered), blood, the flesh of swine, and that on which Allâh's Name has not been mentioned while slaughtering (that which has been slaughtered as a sacrifice for others than Allâh, or has been slaughtered for idols) and that which has been killed by

> strangling, or by a violent blow, or by a headlong fall, or by the goring of horns — and that which has been (partly) eaten by a wild animal — unless you are able to slaughter it (before its death) - and that which is sacrificed (slaughtered) on *An-Nusub* (stone-altars)." (Surah Al-Ma'idah:3)

All the above show that *Shirk* is not confined to worshipping idols and statues. It takes many different forms, all of which have one thing in common: they are all *Haraam*.

Chapter 3

SHIRK IS A GREAT INJUSTICE

﴿وَإِذْ قَالَ لُقْمَٰنُ لِٱبْنِهِۦ وَهُوَ يَعِظُهُۥ يَٰبُنَيَّ لَا تُشْرِكْ بِٱللَّهِ إِنَّ ٱلشِّرْكَ لَظُلْمٌ عَظِيمٌ﴾ [لقمان: ١٣]

"And when Luqman said to his son while advising him: O my son! Do not ascribe partners to Allâh. Indeed *Shirk* is a great injustice." (Surah Luqman:13)

An injustice is to withhold someone's rights or to treat someone in an unfair manner. *Shirk* is thus the greatest injustice. Man considers something which has no power whatsoever to control his life, to be his creator, sustainer and saviour. In praising and worshipping these imaginary deities, he forgets Allâh's sole right to be worshipped. He uses his health, his faculties, all his material earnings and all the amenities that are at his disposal to pray to others. He thus ignores the Creator who has given him the air to breathe, the health to use, the environment to utilise and the wealth to enjoy. He forgets that he is indebted to one being only for everything that he has, the most important of which is his life, and turns to false gods in reverence. He is ungrateful and unjust to his Benevolent and Merciful Creator.

Shirk is an unforgivable sin

﴿إِنَّ ٱللَّهَ لَا يَغْفِرُ أَن يُشْرَكَ بِهِۦ وَيَغْفِرُ مَا دُونَ ذَٰلِكَ لِمَن يَشَآءُ ۚ وَمَن يُشْرِكْ بِٱللَّهِ فَقَدْ ضَلَّ ضَلَٰلًۢا بَعِيدًا﴾ [النساء: ١١٦]

"Indeed Allâh does not forgive joining other gods with Him but He forgives other sins than this of whom He pleases. And the one who joins other gods with Allâh, indeed he has strayed very far away." (Surah An-Nisa:116)

Heaven has been made *Haraam* for those who associate gods with Allâh

﴿ لَقَدْ كَفَرَ ٱلَّذِينَ قَالُوٓاْ إِنَّ ٱللَّهَ هُوَ ٱلْمَسِيحُ ٱبْنُ مَرْيَمَ ۖ وَقَالَ ٱلْمَسِيحُ يَٰبَنِىٓ إِسْرَٰٓءِيلَ ٱعْبُدُواْ ٱللَّهَ رَبِّى وَرَبَّكُمْ ۖ إِنَّهُۥ مَن يُشْرِكْ بِٱللَّهِ فَقَدْ حَرَّمَ ٱللَّهُ عَلَيْهِ ٱلْجَنَّةَ وَمَأْوَىٰهُ ٱلنَّارُ ۖ وَمَا لِلظَّٰلِمِينَ مِنْ أَنصَارٍ ﴾ [المائدة : ٧٢]

"Indeed they do blaspheme who say that Allâh is Christ the son of Mary. But Chirist said: "O Children of Israel! Worship Allâh, my Lord and your Lord." Whoever joins other gods with Allâh — Allâh will forbid him Heaven, and the Fire will be his abode. And there will be no-one to help the wrong-doers." (Surah Al-Ma'idah:72)

All the good deeds of a *Mushrik* are wasted

﴿ وَلَقَدْ أُوحِىَ إِلَيْكَ وَإِلَى ٱلَّذِينَ مِن قَبْلِكَ لَئِنْ أَشْرَكْتَ لَيَحْبَطَنَّ عَمَلُكَ وَلَتَكُونَنَّ مِنَ ٱلْخَٰسِرِينَ ﴾ [الزمر : ٦٥]

"And it was revealed to you (O Muhammad) and to all (the Prophets) before you that if you commit *Shirk*, all your good actions will be wasted and you will be one of the losers." (Surah Az-Zumar:65)

In other words, none of the actions of a *Mushrik* will be regarded as good, none will earn reward for him, and his whole life will have been a waste.

Chapter 4

THE BELIEFS OF A *MUSHRIK* SOCIETY

1. The Arab non-believers had faith in God, but did not accept that He was the sole ruler of the universe.
2. The Jews believed in God, but theirs was a family God who created everything for the Children of Israel, and then settled down to take a well-earned rest.
3. The Christians believed in God, but also maintained that after creating Jesus, He handed over the task of salvation, provision and protection to Jesus, and thus retired from the concerns of mankind.
4. The Persians had accepted the existence of two gods who performed their godly tasks together.
5. The god of the Hindus had managed to splinter himself into many thousands of gods, each with its own scope of work.
6. Some people believed that God needed assistants and courtiers in order to function efficiently.
7. Some believed that God had fallen madly in love with His creation and so, like any lover, allowed them to meddle in His affairs.
8. Others were of the opinion that everything on earth is a part of God Himself.
9. Yet others said that if God is very pleased with one of His creatures, He absorbs that person into Himself so that the worshipper is now part of the worshipped.

Chapter 5

THE PORTRAYAL OF ALLÂH IN THE QUR'AN

1. Allâh is the Creator, Owner, Provider and Ruler of everything.
2. Allâh is eternally present.
3. Allâh is free of all faults, weaknesses and needs.
4. Allâh is Unique and Incomparable. Perceiving Him in His entirety is beyond the limits of the human brain.
5. Allâh has no associates, whether in His person, characteristics, rights or capabilities.

***Shirk* in Allâh's person** (*Shirk against Tawhid al-Asmaa*)

This is to give someone else the same status as Allâh. Examples of this are the Trinity in Christianity, and the belief of the early Arabs that the angels were Allâh's daughters.

***Shirk* in Allâh's attributes** (*Shirk against Tawhid as-Sifat*)

This is to give someone else the qualities and characteristics of Allâh, for example, to think that someone is just as merciful as Allâh.

***Shirk* in Allâh's capabilities** (*Shirk against Tawhid ar-Rububiyya*)

Allâh is capable of doing things which are unique to Him because He is the Lord of the universe. To imagine that someone else can also be capable of such things is *Shirk*. For example, to say that someone other than Allâh can create and provide for his creatures, bless their efforts with success or punish them with loss, is *Shirk*.

***Shirk* in Allâh's Rights** (*Shirk against Tawhid al-Uluhiyya*)

As Lord and Master of the universe, Allâh the Almighty has certain rights which are unique to Him. For example, it is Allâh's right to be the sole object of all worship, whether verbal, physical or material. To redirect worship to someone other than Allâh is to violate this right and so commit *Shirk*. To turn to someone other than Allâh in gratitude for all of one's blessings or to plead for mercy and help in times of hardship is *Shirk*.

Chapter 6

NO COMPARISON BETWEEN THE CREATOR AND HIS CREATION

In describing the nature of Allâh, the Qur'an uses certain words which are used to describe mankind as well. Examples of such words are: compassionate, knowing, hearing and seeing. Some people have thus concluded that mankind, especially the Prophets, has a share in Allâh's characteristics.

Furthermore, they argue that the only difference between the Almighty and mankind is that whereas the characteristics found in Allâh are permanent, the same characteristics found in human beings are only temporary. A Muslim should regard such arguments as nonsensical. There may be a linguistic similarity between the words used for the Creator and His creation, but no more. There is a whole world of difference, for example, between Allâh's Listening and the listening of human beings. Man listens with his ears, but we have no idea of the way in which Allâh listens. Man can only listen to loud noises, while Allâh can hear the heartbeat of a mouse as well as the scampering of an ant.

Man can only hear sounds that are within his range, while there is no limit to the range of sounds that Allâh can hear. Man can only concentrate on one voice at a time, while Allâh can listen and respond to the voices of His millions of creatures, all in the same instance. Man can only hear the sounds of the present, while Allâh hears the sounds of the present, past and future. Man can listen while he is awake, but becomes deaf when sleeping or unconscious. The Almighty has no need for sleep or rest, and He listens to all of His creatures all the time. Man hears just as all other men hear, but Allâh's hearing is unique and complete. It cannot have and does not have any comparison.

The same applies to all of Allâh's attributes that have been compared with the characteristics of mankind. Man can see, but his vision cannot be compared to that of Allâh. Man has organs with which he looks, but we can have no conception of the way in which Allâh looks. Man can only see things in front of him, while Allâh sees everything. Man can only see the external, while Allâh can see all that is internal or hidden. Man can only see appearances and forms, but Allâh can see the thoughts of the mind as well as the feelings of the heart.

The Qur'an thus makes it clear that Allâh's attributes are complete, all-encompassing and incomparable. The *Mushriks* reply, for example, by making a distinction between natural and given knowledge. They say that man's acquired knowledge cannot be compared with that of Allâh, but there are instances in which Allâh gives some of His own unique knowledge to His chosen creatures. These fortunate few are usually Prophets or very pious people. Another example is that the Qur'an says that Allâh alone can see into the future. They accept this, but also add that although no human being can of his own accord look into the future, there are some people who have been blessed by Allâh with the power to do so. Their ability to see into the future is thus not an acquired ability but is given to them by Allâh. Similarly when the verses saying that no-one can harm or benefit others except Allâh are recited to them, they say that they believe in that but add that a human being can have such God-given power.

Such arguments are a fallacy, and they become intolerable when those who advance them claim to be Muslims. It is unfortunate that the Arab unbelievers as well as the Jews and the Christians used to put forward similar arguments in order to justify their false gods. In the following pages, therefore, we will study the beliefs of those non-believers in order to determine whether they thought that the knowledge and power of their gods was given to them by Allâh or was their own. If they too believed that it was given by Allâh, it will be seen that there is no difference between those *Mushriks* and the people of today who advance similar beliefs for their gods and saints. The method of our study is to look at what is refuted in the Qur'an. It is logical to suppose that in the Qur'an, Allâh the Almighty has refuted those practices and beliefs that were actually practised by the people because it would have been useless to negate something which had no existence in the first place.

Chapter 7

THE BELIEFS OF THE ARAB NON-BELIEVERS

1. It is clear in the Qur'an that the early Arabs believed in Allâh and worshipped Him.

﴿ وَلَئِن سَأَلْتَهُم مَّنْ خَلَقَ ٱلسَّمَٰوَٰتِ وَٱلْأَرْضَ وَسَخَّرَ ٱلشَّمْسَ وَٱلْقَمَرَ لَيَقُولُنَّ ٱللَّهُ ۖ فَأَنَّىٰ يُؤْفَكُونَ ﴾ [العنكبوت : ٦١]

"And if you ask them, who created the heavens and the earth and made the sun and the moon subservient, they will certainly reply, "Allâh". So how are they then deluded away?" (Al-Ankabut:61)

2. The Arabs used to worship their false gods not because they considered them to be Allâh but because they considered them to be intermediaries.

﴿ أَلَا لِلَّهِ ٱلدِّينُ ٱلْخَالِصُ ۚ وَٱلَّذِينَ ٱتَّخَذُوا۟ مِن دُونِهِۦٓ أَوْلِيَآءَ مَا نَعْبُدُهُمْ إِلَّا لِيُقَرِّبُونَآ إِلَى ٱللَّهِ زُلْفَىٰٓ إِنَّ ٱللَّهَ يَحْكُمُ بَيْنَهُمْ فِى مَا هُمْ فِيهِ يَخْتَلِفُونَ ۗ إِنَّ ٱللَّهَ لَا يَهْدِى مَنْ هُوَ كَٰذِبٌ كَفَّارٌ ﴾ [الزمر : ٣]

"But those who take for protectors other than Allâh say: We only serve them in order that they may bring us nearer to Allâh." (Az-Zumar:3)

3. The Arabs also worshipped their deities so that they may intercede on behalf of them in front of Allâh.

﴿ وَيَعْبُدُونَ مِن دُونِ ٱللَّهِ مَا لَا يَضُرُّهُمْ وَلَا يَنفَعُهُمْ وَيَقُولُونَ هَٰٓؤُلَآءِ شُفَعَٰٓؤُنَا عِندَ ٱللَّهِ ۚ قُلْ أَتُنَبِّـُٔونَ ٱللَّهَ بِمَا لَا يَعْلَمُ فِى ٱلسَّمَٰوَٰتِ وَلَا فِى ٱلْأَرْضِ ۚ سُبْحَٰنَهُۥ وَتَعَٰلَىٰ عَمَّا يُشْرِكُونَ ﴾ [يونس : ١٨]

"And they worship, besides Allâh, those that do not hurt them or profit them, and they say: These are our intercessors with Allâh." (Yunus:18)

4. The Arabs considered their gods to be their helpers and providers only while on dry land. When in the sea, they appealed to Allâh the Almighty alone.

﴿ فَإِذَا رَكِبُوا۟ فِى ٱلْفُلْكِ دَعَوُا۟ ٱللَّهَ مُخْلِصِينَ لَهُ ٱلدِّينَ فَلَمَّا نَجَّىٰهُمْ إِلَى ٱلْبَرِّ إِذَا هُمْ يُشْرِكُونَ ﴾ [العنكبوت: ٦٥]

"If they embark on a boat, they call on Allâh, making their devotion sincerely to Him. But when He has delivered them on dry land, behold! They commit *Shirk*." (Al-Ankabut:65)

5. It is thus very clear that the *Mushrik* Arabs considered their Prophets, saints, angels, jinns and other gods to be mere intercessors on behalf of them in the court of Allâh Almighty. They believed that these gods could not of their own accord provide sustenance, health or good fortune. Instead, they acted as intermediaries between mankind and Allâh. It is reported in a Hadith that these Arabs used to recite the following words when circling the Ka'ba:

"Here I am, O Lord! Here I am. You have no partner, except the partner who is Yours. You own him and You own all that he owns."

Similarly, the Jews believed that the Prophet Uzair عليه السلام had no special qualities of his own except those that were given to him as a son by Allâh. The Christians gave a similar status to Prophet 'Isa عليه السلام.

6. The Qur'an expressly denies that Allâh gave any of His Prophets or pious people any knowledge or power that was His alone. There were incidents in which some of the Prophets were able to do fantastic things (such as Prophet 'Isa healing the lepers and the blind), but these were miracles. None of the Prophets, for example, was given the power to see into the future. There were instances in which Allâh told His Messengers about certain things that were

going to happen, but He did not give them the complete ability to see into the future for themselves.

﴿ قُل لَّآ أَمۡلِكُ لِنَفۡسِي ضَرّٗا وَلَا نَفۡعًا إِلَّا مَا شَآءَ ٱللَّهُۗ ﴾ [يونس : ٤٩]

"Say: I have no power over any harm or profit to myself except as Allâh wills." (Yunus:49)

This means that the Prophet has no power (whether his own or God-given) over any harm or gain. Whatever happens to him, happens by the will of Allâh.

﴿ قُل لَّا يَعۡلَمُ مَن فِي ٱلسَّمَٰوَٰتِ وَٱلۡأَرۡضِ ٱلۡغَيۡبَ إِلَّا ٱللَّهُۚ وَمَا يَشۡعُرُونَ أَيَّانَ يُبۡعَثُونَ ﴾

[النمل : ٦٥]

"Say: None in the heavens or the earth knows what is hidden, except Allâh. Nor can they perceive when they shall be raised up (for Judgment)." (An-Namal:65)

In other words, no-one has any knowledge whatsoever, whether of his own or God-given, about the hidden and about the future.

To summarize, there are some characteristics which Allâh and His creatures seem to share, such as the ability to see and the ability to hear. But our discussion has shown that any similarity is superficial and that there is a great deal of difference between the two. There are other characteristics which belong to Allâh Almighty alone, and no human being has ever been given a share of these abilities. These include the knowledge of the unseen and absolute power.

Chapter 8

EVERYTHING IS IN THE HANDS OF ALLÂH

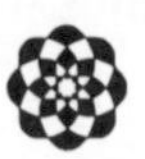

1. Allâh alone is responsible for life and death.

﴿ كَيْفَ تَكْفُرُونَ بِاللَّهِ وَكُنتُمْ أَمْوَاتًا فَأَحْيَاكُمْ ثُمَّ يُمِيتُكُمْ ثُمَّ يُحْيِيكُمْ ثُمَّ إِلَيْهِ تُرْجَعُونَ ﴾ [البقرة: ٢٨]

"How can you reject faith in Allâh? Seeing that you were without life and He gave you life. Then He will cause you to die and He will again bring you to life, and again to Him you will return." (Al-Baqarah:28)

2. He is the only one who can answer the prayers of the needy and the sick.

﴿ أَمَّن يُجِيبُ الْمُضْطَرَّ إِذَا دَعَاهُ وَيَكْشِفُ السُّوءَ وَيَجْعَلُكُمْ خُلَفَاءَ الْأَرْضِ أَإِلَٰهٌ مَّعَ اللَّهِ ﴾ [النمل: ٦٢]

Is not He (better than your gods) Who responds to the distressed one, when he calls on Him, and Who removes the evil, and makes you inheritors of the earth, generations after generations? Is there any *ilâh* (god) with Allâh??" (An-Namal:62)

This was Prophet Ibrahim's prayer:

﴿ الَّذِي خَلَقَنِي فَهُوَ يَهْدِينِ ○ وَالَّذِي هُوَ يُطْعِمُنِي وَيَسْقِينِ ○ وَإِذَا مَرِضْتُ فَهُوَ يَشْفِينِ ○ وَالَّذِي يُمِيتُنِي ثُمَّ يُحْيِينِ ○ وَالَّذِي أَطْمَعُ أَن يَغْفِرَ لِي خَطِيئَتِي يَوْمَ الدِّينِ ﴾ [الشعراء: ٧٨-٨٢]

"The One Who created me, it is He Who guides me. And it is He Who gives me food and drink. And when I am ill, it is He Who cures me. And Who will cause me to die and then to live again. And Who, I hope, will forgive me my faults on the Day of Judgment.” (Ash-Shu‘arâ: 78-82)

3. Our prayers for children should be directed to Him alone, not to dead saints in their tombs.

﴿ لِّلَّهِ مُلْكُ ٱلسَّمَٰوَٰتِ وَٱلْأَرْضِ ۚ يَخْلُقُ مَا يَشَآءُ ۚ يَهَبُ لِمَن يَشَآءُ إِنَٰثًا وَيَهَبُ لِمَن يَشَآءُ ٱلذُّكُورَ ۝ أَوْ يُزَوِّجُهُمْ ذُكْرَانًا وَإِنَٰثًا ۖ وَيَجْعَلُ مَن يَشَآءُ عَقِيمًا ۚ ﴾

[الشورى : ٤٩-٥٠]

“To Allâh belong the heavens and the earth. He creates what He wills. He gives daughters to whom He wills and gives sons to whom He wills. Or He gives them sons and daughters. And He leaves barren whom He wills. (Ash-Shu‘arâ: 49,50)

Prophet Ibrahim عليه السلام prayed to Allâh:

﴿ رَبِّ هَبْ لِى مِنَ ٱلصَّٰلِحِينَ ﴾ [الصافات : ١٠٠]

“O Lord! Grant me (a son) from among the righteous.” (As-Sâffât: 100)

4. He is the Sustainer and Provider for all creatures.

﴿ وَيَعْبُدُونَ مِن دُونِ ٱللَّهِ مَا لَا يَمْلِكُ لَهُمْ رِزْقًا مِّنَ ٱلسَّمَٰوَٰتِ وَٱلْأَرْضِ شَيْـًٔا وَلَا يَسْتَطِيعُونَ ﴾ [النحل : ٧٣]

“And they worship, instead of Allâh, those that have no power to provide them with sustenance from the heavens and the earth, and cannot possibly have such power.” (An-Nahl: 73)

5. Honour and disgrace are in His Power to give.

﴿ قُلِ ٱللَّهُمَّ مَٰلِكَ ٱلْمُلْكِ تُؤْتِى ٱلْمُلْكَ مَن تَشَآءُ وَتَنزِعُ ٱلْمُلْكَ مِمَّن تَشَآءُ وَتُعِزُّ مَن تَشَآءُ وَتُذِلُّ مَن تَشَآءُ ۖ بِيَدِكَ ٱلْخَيْرُ ۖ إِنَّكَ عَلَىٰ كُلِّ شَىْءٍ قَدِيرٌ ﴾

[آل عمران : ٢٦]

"Say: O Allâh! Lord of power. You give power to whom You please, and You remove from power whom You please. You give honour to whom You please and You disgrace whom You please. In Your hand is all Good. Indeed, over all things You have power." (Âl-Imran:26)

6. Forgiveness for sins should be pleaded only at His door-step.

﴿نَبِّئْ عِبَادِىٓ أَنِّىٓ أَنَا ٱلْغَفُورُ ٱلرَّحِيمُ ۝ وَأَنَّ عَذَابِى هُوَ ٱلْعَذَابُ ٱلْأَلِيمُ﴾ [الحجر: ٤٩-٥٠]

"Inform my servants that I am the Forgiver, the Merciful, and that My punishment is a very severe punishment." (Al-Hijr: 49,50)

Chapter 9

MAN AND HIS NEEDS

Our needs as human beings are numerous and diverse. They revolve around our spiritual and physical health, food and clothing, possessions and wealth, family and friends, honour and freedom. Our outer and inner worlds are affecting us constantly, creating needs that have to be fulfilled and problems that have to be solved. We need food when hungry, cures for diseases, children to love, friends to talk to, hobbies to relieve boredom, and much, much more. But things go wrong all the time. Friendships break, jobs are lost, loved ones fall ill. We need help, both physical and spiritual, and so we turn to someone stronger than ourselves in prayer.

Allâh Almighty has created the world to serve us. He has made provisions for all our needs. They include the sun, the rains, the mountains, the vegetation, the land and the animals. All of them remain under his strict control and cannot conceivably do anything that he does not command.

Why then do we pray to a dead man in his grave for rain, when the one who controls the rains is there to be asked? Why do we pray to a human being for children, when there is a Creator Who alone gives life and alone causes death?

When a person prays, whether to a tree, angel, Prophet or saint, he does so because he needs something or because he wants to show his gratitude. He believes that the object of his worship is in a position to help him. People appeal to Shaikh Abdul Qadir, to the Buddha, to Krishna, to Jesus or to Prophet Muhammad (صلى الله عليه وسلم). Some sailors evoke the name of Khwaja Mueenud-din Chishti to reach the shore safely. Human beings, dead and alive, have acquired reputations for extreme piety and divinity. If living, they are followed by hundreds of their admiring devotees. If dead, their graves have become places of pilgrimage and prayer.

A ludicrous contradiction we see in our countries is the sight of people praying for children and health at the tombs of their saints. If such 'holy' men did have the ability to give life and health, would they not have practised these coveted talents on themselves first? Would they not have exchanged the dark and narrow world of the grave for the wide, open spaces of the earth? Would they not have exchanged the grim helplessness of death for the happy activity of life?

Can a human fulfill our needs?

We do not deny that a person can fulfill the needs of another person. The person, who feeds someone, nurses the patient or releases the prisoner, is fulfilling their needs. A shoemaker fulfills the need for shoes, the tailor provides clothes and the driver provides transport. We human beings not only benefit from each other but from other things as well. Trees provide life-saving shelter from the burning rays of the sun. Horses and camels can be invaluable to travellers. We need needles to sew and scissors to cut. If we thus look around us, we will see that most of our time is spent in trying to make our own lives easier. The car has been invented, but that is not enough; each new model of car has to be better and faster than the last. Few household tasks are performed today without the use of a machine. Computers are being used in many areas to provide speed and efficiency. But despite our total reliance on all these gadgets and machines, we cannot say that they are god-like. They are almost indispensable to us today — that is true, but that does not make them divine. No matter how efficient and useful a machine is, all the credit of its work goes to its designer. In the same way, no matter how strong or helpful a person is, the credit should go to Allâh.

If we could prove that a certain person had an influence in the creation of the world, we could call him our sustainer and provider. But when it is clear that every minute particle existing in the universe has been created by Allâh, such a claim becomes a clear lie.

It is a sheer fallacy to suppose that an insignificant human being could have had a share in the creation of the universe. *Mushrik* nations like the Hindus and the Buddhists have adopted the belief that just as Allâh is the Provider and Helper, so the saints and legendary heroes were providers and helpers. Allâh gave them a spark of His own divinity so that they could share in His great work.

Such a belief is a lie and a distortion. It is completely alien to the teachings of Islam and is an insult to the majesty and power of Allâh the Almighty. He alone created the heavens, the earth, and everything that lies between them. He alone has power and control over everything. He alone gives life and He alone causes death, whether of an ant or of a superpower president. The drought that destroys lives, the tornadoes that wreck harvests, the hurricanes that annihilate cities — all are under the command of Allâh.

He first created the perfect environment in which mankind could live, providing for warmth, food and water, livelihood and pleasure. But He did not leave His creatures alone and at the mercy of Satan after this. He provided for continuous guidance and example through his numerous Prophets and Messengers. Again and again He stressed that He is there to help His creatures and to answer their prayers and appeals. To ignore all He has said and turn in prayer to human beings, trees and angels, is an affront to the dignity of the Lord, Creator and Preserver of the universe.

A *Mushrik* would justify himself by saying that gods and saints can fulfill the needs of those in distress, not on their own but by the power that Allâh has given to them. Such a belief is not in accordance with the teachings contained in the Qur'an and Sunnah. We will now give an illustration from the Qur'an to show the difference between help given by Allâh and help given by an ordinary human being. Once this difference has been clarified, there will be no excuse left to believe that deities and saints can share in the attributes that belong to Allâh alone.

The story of Musa (Moses) in Madyan

﴿ وَلَمَّا تَوَجَّهَ تِلْقَاءَ مَدْيَنَ قَالَ عَسَىٰ رَبِّي أَن يَهْدِيَنِي سَوَاءَ السَّبِيلِ ۝ وَلَمَّا وَرَدَ مَاءَ مَدْيَنَ وَجَدَ عَلَيْهِ أُمَّةً مِّنَ النَّاسِ يَسْقُونَ وَوَجَدَ مِن دُونِهِمُ امْرَأَتَيْنِ تَذُودَانِ ۖ قَالَ مَا خَطْبُكُمَا ۖ قَالَتَا لَا نَسْقِي حَتَّىٰ يُصْدِرَ الرِّعَاءُ ۖ وَأَبُونَا شَيْخٌ كَبِيرٌ ۝ فَسَقَىٰ لَهُمَا ﴾ [القصص : ٢٢-٢٤]

"Then, when he turned his face towards (the land of) Madyan, he said: I do hope my Lord will show me the smooth and straight path. And when he arrived at the watering place in Madyan, he found there a group of men watering their flocks, and besides them he found two women who were keeping back (their flock). He said: What is the matter with you? They said: We cannot water our flocks until the shepherds take back their flocks. And our father is a very old man. So he watered their flock for them." (Al-Qasas: 22-24)

According to some narrations, Musa (عليه السلام), motivated by sympathy for the girls, went to another well which was covered by a heavy stone. He lifted the stone and drew water for the girls and their flock. The need of the girls was thus fulfilled, and let us now discuss the story to see the factors which helped to fulfill their need.

We can say that the water quenched their thirst because this is the natural method of alleviating thirst. We can also say that Musa (عليه السلام) quenched their thirst as he was the one who lifted the heavy stone and drew the water. But we can just as correctly say that Allâh quenched their thirst because He is the One Who created water. He gave it the quality of alleviating thirst, and He is the One Who created Musa عليه السلام and gave him the power to lift that heavy stone.

So water was the direct factor that met their need, Musa (عليه السلام) was the indirect factor, and Allâh was the Creator of all these factors. Mankind thus has some power to help itself and help others, but the real source of all this aid is Allâh alone. He creates mankind, He creates all the circumstances that surround mankind, and He gives mankind the ability to help itself. Without Allâh, we are utterly powerless and helpless.

Chapter 10

PRAYERS FOR MIRACLES

The object of prayer is not that man prays while Allâh does everything for him. Prayer is an appeal to Allâh to help the person in his trials, ease his sufferings and reward his actions. Remember: Allâh helps those who help themselves. Allâh has given us our hands and feet, our senses and faculties, our intelligence and capabilities to be used and not to trust. When we ask Allâh for something, we are asking Him to help create the environment in which our needs can be fulfilled. When we pray for food, we are not expecting to find plates of rice and meat descending from the sky. What we want is that Allâh help us to find a job, earn a living and be able to provide for ourselves.

Prayer should be accompanied by action. It is no use sitting at home doing nothing, and then praying to Allâh to help you get a job. Consider the following person:

He avoids water, and prays to Allâh to quench his thirst. He closes his eyes, and prays to Allâh to help him see. He plants an apple tree, and prays for wheat. He remains celibate and longs for children. He opposes the Qur'an and Sunnah, and then prays for guidance. He indulges in unforgivable sins, and then prays for heaven. Such a person will be considered foolish as he is defying divine justice and logic.

﴿ وَأَن لَّيْسَ لِلْإِنسَٰنِ إِلَّا مَا سَعَىٰ ﴾ [النجم: ٣٩]

"Man can have nothing but what he strives for." (An-Najam: 39)

It is also important to remember that prayers should not be for illegitimate or un-reasonable things. It is useless to pray to Allâh to restore your dead relative back to life as this is not the plan that Allâh has for His creation. Most important of all, prayers should be addressed directly to Allâh Almighty only. If a person prays via the intercession of a saint or Prophet, he should not be surprised that the Lord of the universe does not respond to him. An illustration from the battle of *Uhud* will help clarify the relation between cause and effect.

The battle of *Uhud*

This battle is an example of the Muslims not being helped by Allâh because they disobeyed the command of Allâh's Messenger. In the third year after Hijra, the Makkans attacked the Muslims with an army of three thousand men, seven hundred of which were in armour. The Muslim army was composed of only one thousand men, three hundred of which were hypocrites who deserted the Muslims before the battle began.

Allâh's Messenger صلى الله عليه وسلم stationed fifty archers on a hill to guard the rear of the Muslim lines. This was a strategically crucial position and the Prophet صلى الله عليه وسلم stressed that under no circumstances were the men to move from their position.

> "Do not desert your positions — even if you see vultures snatching at our bones."

When the fighting began, the Muslims clearly had the advantage. Panic and fear broke out among the Makkan army as more and more of its men were killed. It slowly took to flight and the Muslims began to gather the booty. Seeing this, the forty archers left their posts and rushed towards the spoils of war. The retreating Makkan army took advantage of this lapse in security and counter-attacked. The Muslims were taken by surprise and so suffered a huge loss. Seventy of the Companions were martyred, including the Prophet's beloved uncle, Hamza رضي الله عنه.

The Prophet صلى الله عليه وسلم was himself surrounded by the enemy. Stones, arrows and spears rained down upon him. His face and head were badly injured, covering his body in blood. Allâh's Messenger صلى الله عليه وسلم fell in a ditch and was surrounded by the enemies of Islam who joyfully shouted, "Muhammad has been killed!"

But Allâh's Messenger صلى الله عليه وسلم emerged from the ditch in wounded state, his voice thundering above the noise of the battle.

> "I am the Prophet. There is no doubt about this. I am the son of Abdul Muttalib."

His words brought courage into the hearts of his followers and they returned to the fighting with renewed vigour. As the Prophet (صلى الله عليه وسلم) was still surrounded by the enemy, he shouted to his devoted men, "Whoever removes them away from me, for him is Paradise."

The Ansari youth fell on the Makkans circling the Prophet صلى الله عليه وسلم like tigers. They were immediately slaughtered by the more experienced Makkans, but as they lay dying at the Prophet's feet, each said with deep contentment, "By the Lord of the Ka'ba, I leave the world successfully."

Each one of them had coveted the status of a martyr. And each left the world in blissful anticipation of the reward that Allâh had promised them. Theirs was true faith and piety.

As a result of such courage and devotion, the Muslims were still able to save the day.

But had the archers not disobeyed their orders, such a heavy price may not have had to be paid. Despite the fact that Allâh's Messenger (صلى الله عليه وسلم) was himself present in this battle along with some of the most noble and virtuous Companions, the Muslims suffered heavy losses and could have been annihilated completely. The mistake was that of a handful of men, but the entire existing Muslim Ummah could have suffered the effects of this mistake.

This shows that Allâh's promise of help and aid is only for those who obey His commands and follow the Sunnah of His Messenger (صلى الله عليه وسلم). No amount of prayers and supplications will be of use if His commands are not obeyed.

To abandon prayer is *Kufr*

At the same time we should not underestimate the importance of prayer in the eyes of Allâh. Allâh wants us to work hard, but He also wants us to turn to Him in humility and prayer. The person who uses his talents and all the means at his disposal, should not become vain and expect success at once. He should remember that success and failure are both in the hands of Allâh, and prayer should become an integral part of his life.

﴿ أَمَّن يُجِيبُ ٱلْمُضْطَرَّ إِذَا دَعَاهُ وَيَكْشِفُ ٱلسُّوٓءَ وَيَجْعَلُكُمْ خُلَفَآءَ ٱلْأَرْضِ ۗ أَءِلَٰهٌ مَّعَ ٱللَّهِ ۚ قَلِيلًا مَّا تَذَكَّرُونَ ﴾ [النمل : ٦٢]

"Or, who listens to the distressed soul when it calls on Him, and who relieves its suffering, and makes you (mankind) inheritors of the earth? Can there be another god except Allâh? Little it is that you heed." (An-Namal: 62)

Allâh Almighty asks three questions in this verse:

1. When a person is in desperate need and feels helpless from all sources, who is it that alone listens to his prayers and responds to him?
2. When a person is overwhelmed by a problem, who is it that solves his problem and eases his suffering?
3. Who is it that created mankind and then created everything that mankind would need?

Allâh Almighty then answers these questions, saying that He alone is the Creator, the One Who listens and the One Who helps. He then asks us why we turn to others for help, when He is there to answer our prayers.

Chapter 11

THE EMERGENCE OF SHIRK

There are three basic reasons behind the emergence of *Kufr* and *Shirk* practices: an incorrect concept of Allâh, incorrect concept of worship, and an incorrect understanding of the relation between the Creator and His creation. In the following pages we will discuss some of these misguided concepts, explaining them in the correct light of the Qur'an and Sunnah.

Kinship between Allâh and His Creation

Some people suggest that very pious and devout people become so close to Allâh that He treats them as his own sons, wives or daughters. Conversely speaking, these 'relatives' of Allâh are able to change and influence His actions just as a wife may influence her husband or a son may influence his father. Such people are obviously in a position of considerable power, and so to pray to them rather than to Allâh Almighty directly is just as rewarding. The Qur'an has forcefully rejected this concept.

﴿وَأَنَّهُۥ تَعَٰلَىٰ جَدُّ رَبِّنَا مَا ٱتَّخَذَ صَٰحِبَةً وَلَا وَلَدًا﴾ [الجن: ٣]

"And exalted is the Majesty of our Lord: He has taken neither a wife nor a son." (Al-Jinn: 3)

In another place we read:

﴿وَقَالَتِ ٱلْيَهُودُ عُزَيْرٌ ٱبْنُ ٱللَّهِ وَقَالَتِ ٱلنَّصَٰرَى ٱلْمَسِيحُ ٱبْنُ ٱللَّهِ ۖ ذَٰلِكَ قَوْلُهُم بِأَفْوَٰهِهِمْ ۖ يُضَٰهِـُٔونَ قَوْلَ ٱلَّذِينَ كَفَرُوا۟ مِن قَبْلُ ۚ قَٰتَلَهُمُ ٱللَّهُ ۚ أَنَّىٰ يُؤْفَكُونَ﴾ [التوبة: ٣٠]

"The Jews say Uzair is the son of Allâh, and the Christians say Christ is the son of Allâh. This is a saying from their mouth; in this they but imitate what the unbelievers of old used to say. Allâh's curse be upon them; how they are deluded away from the truth!" (At-Taubah: 30)

The belief that Allâh regards the angels as His daughters has also been rejected.

﴿أَفَأَصْفَىٰكُمْ رَبُّكُم بِٱلْبَنِينَ وَٱتَّخَذَ مِنَ ٱلْمَلَٰٓئِكَةِ إِنَٰثًا ۚ إِنَّكُمْ لَتَقُولُونَ قَوْلًا عَظِيمًا﴾

[بني إسرائيل : ٤٠]

"Has then your Lord preferred for you sons, and taken for Himself daughters among the angels? Truly you utter a most dreadful saying!" (Bani Israel: 40)

Allâh's infatuation with His creation

A similar belief is that when a person becomes so devout that he has absolutely no interest left in the concerns of the world, Allâh Almighty not only falls madly in love with him but is completely and utterly infatuated by him. And like any mortal lover, Allâh Almighty is prepared to grant any whim and any wish of His beloved. These beloved are thus in a position to plead for forgiveness for their followers who pray to them.

This belief is utterly without foundation and it is an insult to our Creator. Passionate love and infatuation are faults found among mankind which make them blind to reality and justice. Allâh Almighty is above such base human emotions and He is perfect. When describing the relationship between the Creator and His creation, the Qur'an and Sunnah have used the concept of love. But Allâh's love is like all His other characteristics: it is pure, unique, and impossible for the mortal mind to comprehend fully. The fact that Allâh loves someone simply means that Allâh guides him, forgives his faults and gives him success in this world and in the Hereafter.

The concept of *Tawassul* (Intercession)

As discussed earlier, the *Mushrik* Arabs used to worship Allâh, but they also honoured and worshipped Prophets, angels, jinns and various other deities. They worshipped all these creatures not because they considered them to be Allâh but because they considered them to be intercessors in the court of Allâh.

﴿وَلَئِن سَأَلْتَهُم مَّنْ خَلَقَ السَّمَوَاتِ وَالْأَرْضَ وَسَخَّرَ الشَّمْسَ وَالْقَمَرَ لَيَقُولُنَّ اللَّهُ فَأَنَّى يُؤْفَكُونَ﴾ [العنكبوت: ٦١]

"If indeed you ask them: Who has created the heavens and the earth, and subjected the sun and the moon. They will certainly reply, Allâh. How are they then deluded away from the truth?" (Al-Ankabut: 61)

These and other verses of the Qur'an show the following:

1. The Arab un-believers believed in Allâh but also believed in other deities which were supposed to have the role of intercessors.
2. There is no difference between worshipping a deity as God or worshipping it as an intercessor, and both are *Haraam*.
3. Worshipping someone other than Allâh can never be a way of winning Allâh's pleasure as it is *Shirk*, and *Shirk* only invites Allâh's wrath.
4. Allâh listens to all of His creatures all the time, regardless of the language they speak. His throne is guarded by no gurads and no gatekeepers; there are no lawyers and no interpreters in His court. He directly listens and responds to all of His creation.
5. People have invented the concept of using Prophets and saints as intercessors, but they have never been able to agree on the same intercessors. There is severe animosity between the followers of the various saints. Not only every town, but every village and every community has its own mentors.

6. Allâh Almighty has never told us to worship creatures other than Him. In fact He has expressly forbidden it, just as the Prophets and the very saints, who are being worshipped, have forbidden it.

7. And Allâh has never told us to pray to Him invoking the name of a dead saint. It is, however, acceptable to invoke the name of a pious servant of Allâh who is alive and has agreed to praying on your behalf. People usually ignore this requirement and invoke the memories of the dead who have no idea that they are thus being remembered. Their graves have become places of mediation, although the Qur'an tells us,

﴿ يَٰٓأَيُّهَا ٱلَّذِينَ ءَامَنُواْ ٱتَّقُواْ ٱللَّهَ وَٱبۡتَغُوٓاْ إِلَيۡهِ ٱلۡوَسِيلَةَ ﴾

[المائدة : ٣٥]

"O you who believe! Fear Allâh and seek the means of approach to Him." (Al-Mâ'idah:35)

﴿ قُلۡ إِن كُنتُمۡ تُحِبُّونَ ٱللَّهَ فَٱتَّبِعُونِي يُحۡبِبۡكُمُ ٱللَّهُ وَيَغۡفِرۡ لَكُمۡ ذُنُوبَكُمۡۚ وَٱللَّهُ غَفُورٞ رَّحِيمٞ ﴾

[آل عمران : ٣١]

"Say: If you do love Allâh, follow me: Allâh will love you and forgive your sins, and Allâh is Forgiving, Most Merciful." (Âl-Imran: 31)

It is thus clear that the intercession we have been told to find is total adherence to the Prophet's (صلى الله عليه وسلم) message. The one, who ignores this source of mediation, will permanently be astray.

Allâh Almighty has no need for mediators

Mushrik nations have compared Allâh's rule to the rule of ordinary kings. They think that just because mortal rulers need officials, guards and advisors to run their tiny empires, so Allâh needs a retinue of officials to help control the universe. Such comparisons are offensive to Allâh as they belittle His power and bring Him down to the level of insignificant human beings. Allâh

Almighty is incomparable and His method of rule is perfect and incomparable as well.

﴿ فَلَا تَضْرِبُوا۟ لِلَّهِ ٱلْأَمْثَالَ ۚ إِنَّ ٱللَّهَ يَعْلَمُ وَأَنتُمْ لَا تَعْلَمُونَ ﴾ [النحل : ٧٤]

"Invent not similitudes for Allâh: for Allâh knows, and you know not." (An-Nahl: 74)

The practice of praying to Prophets and saints in order to win their intercession in front of Allâh has been denounced as *Shirk* in the Qur'an.

﴿ فَلَوْلَا نَصَرَهُمُ ٱلَّذِينَ ٱتَّخَذُوا۟ مِن دُونِ ٱللَّهِ قُرْبَانًا ءَالِهَةًۢ ۖ بَلْ ضَلُّوا۟ عَنْهُمْ ۚ وَذَٰلِكَ إِفْكُهُمْ وَمَا كَانُوا۟ يَفْتَرُونَ ﴾ [الأحقاف : ٢٨]

"Why then was there no help from those whom they worshipped instead of Allâh, as a means of access to Allâh? Indeed, they left them in the lurch: That was their falsehood and their invention." (Al-Ahqaf: 28)

Worthless were the magnificent tombs built to win the intercession of the dead; wasted were the gifts to the memories of saints; useless were the chants in the names of various deities. When Allâh sent down His hurricanes and floods, all the false gods and supposed mediators were annihilated along with their followers. This was because the whole building of *Tawassul* and *Shirk* was built on a foundation of lies and distortion and so brought the wrath of Allâh on its constructors.

The annals of history record the story of the Muslims of Bukhara immediately after World War 1 when they were told of an impending attack by the socialist forces. Instead of preparing a defense as the Qur'an instructs Muslims to do, these misled people replied, "Shah Naqshaband is the guardian of this country and no enemy will ever conquer it." History is a living proof that in 1920 the Bolsheviks attacked this country, demolished its mosques, slaughtered its scholars, imprisoned its inhabitants, and so brought three hundred magnificent years of Muslim rule to a sudden end. Today, almost seventy years later, the Muslims are still under the yoke of Communist rule, unable to free themselves.

Ignorance

When such misguided people saw the brilliant sun that is essential for plant growth, the clouds that send life-giving rain, the trees that provide fruit, they assumed that these were the gods of nourishment and so forgot the real Nourisher and Provider.

When these people saw the ferocious animals that can tear man from limb to limb, the erupting volcanoes that can destroy entire villages, the diseases and plagues that bring mankind down to its knees, their fear knew no bounds. In order to appease these angry and destructive gods, they built memorials in their name to which they sacrificed and offered gifts. Their state of fear was such that they bowed in worship to anything and everything, to the extent that they almost lost count of the number of their gods.

And when these people saw the miracles of the Prophets, they assumed that these were divine characters who had influence over the running of the world.

Allâh Almighty has rejected all such beliefs and has stated the following in order to guide His creatures:

﴿فَسُبْحَـٰنَ ٱلَّذِى بِيَدِهِۦ مَلَكُوتُ كُلِّ شَىْءٍ وَإِلَيْهِ تُرْجَعُونَ﴾ [يس : ٨٣]

"So glory to Him in Whose hands is the dominion of all things: and to Him will you all be brought back." (Ya Sin: 83)

Everything is under the total control of Allâh

The first thing taught by Islam is that nothing in the universe can of its own will harm or benefit man. Each and every drop of water, each grain of sand, each leaf on a tree is under the command of the Creator who formed it and gave it life.

Mankind is the best creation of Allâh

Islam gives human beings the birth-right of being the best creation of Allâh, better than the rest of creation. It is because of his actions that man falls to the lowest of the low.

﴿۞ وَلَقَدْ كَرَّمْنَا بَنِيٓ ءَادَمَ وَحَمَلْنَٰهُمْ فِي ٱلْبَرِّ وَٱلْبَحْرِ وَرَزَقْنَٰهُم مِّنَ ٱلطَّيِّبَٰتِ وَفَضَّلْنَٰهُمْ عَلَىٰ كَثِيرٖ مِّمَّنْ خَلَقْنَا تَفْضِيلٗا﴾ [بني إسرائيل : ٧٠]

"We have honoured the sons of Adam; provided them with transport on land and sea; given them for sustenance things good and pure; and favoured them over a great part of Our creation." (Bani Israel: 70)

Mankind has no lord or master except Allâh

﴿وَمِنْ ءَايَٰتِهِ ٱلَّيْلُ وَٱلنَّهَارُ وَٱلشَّمْسُ وَٱلْقَمَرُۚ لَا تَسْجُدُواْ لِلشَّمْسِ وَلَا لِلْقَمَرِ وَٱسْجُدُواْۤ لِلَّهِ ٱلَّذِي خَلَقَهُنَّ إِن كُنتُمْ إِيَّاهُ تَعْبُدُونَ﴾

[فصلت : ٣٧]

"And from among His signs are the night and the day, and the sun and the moon. Prostrate not to the sun not to the moon but prostrate to Allâh Who created them, if it is Him you wish to worship." (Fussilat: 37)

The Prophets are the creatures of Allâh

Islam has taught that the Prophets and Messengers were ordinary human beings who were chosen to receive and spread the faith of Allâh. They had to devote their lives to the worship of Allâh just as all other human beings are required to do.

﴿إِن كُلُّ مَن فِي ٱلسَّمَٰوَٰتِ وَٱلْأَرْضِ إِلَّآ ءَاتِي ٱلرَّحْمَٰنِ عَبْدٗا﴾ [مريم : ٩٣]

"All that is in the heavens and the earth must come to Allâh Most Gracious as a servant." (Maryam: 93)

Miracles are the work of Allâh alone

The fifth lesson given by Islam is that miracles performed by Prophets are not their works but are the acts of Allâh. He uses miracles to show the truth of the message being preached by His servants.

﴿ وَلَقَدْ أَرْسَلْنَا رُسُلًا مِّن قَبْلِكَ وَجَعَلْنَا لَهُمْ أَزْوَاجًا وَذُرِّيَّةً وَمَا كَانَ لِرَسُولٍ أَن يَأْتِيَ بِآيَةٍ إِلَّا بِإِذْنِ ٱللَّهِ لِكُلِّ أَجَلٍ كِتَابٌ ﴾ [الرعد: ٣٨]

"We did send Messengers before you, and appointed for them wives and children. And it was never the part of a Messenger to bring a sign except as Allâh permitted. For each period is a Book (revealed). (Ar-Ra'd: 38)

In the Qur'an the word "sign" signifies a miracle. During the mission of the Prophet Muhammad (صلى الله عليه وسلم) the Arab non-believers demanded that he perform a miracle if he was a true Prophet in the tradition of Prophet Musa who performed the miracles of the parting of the seas and the white hand, and Prophet 'Isa who healed the lepers and the blind. Allâh the Almighty answered these people by saying that Prophets had no control over His miracles and that He only performed them when He so wished.

﴿ فَلَمْ تَقْتُلُوهُمْ وَلَٰكِنَّ ٱللَّهَ قَتَلَهُمْ وَمَا رَمَيْتَ إِذْ رَمَيْتَ وَلَٰكِنَّ ٱللَّهَ رَمَىٰ ﴾ [الأنفال: ١٧]

"It is not you who slew them but Allâh slew them; when you threw (a handful of dust) it was not your act, but Allâh's." (Al-Anfal: 17)

The verses refer to the battle between the Muslims and non-Muslims, at the beginning of which the Prophet صلى الله عليه وسلم threw a fistful of sand towards the non-believers shouting "May their faces become disfigured.' At the same time, he gave the order for the battle to commence; and the Companions threw themselves into the fighting with such vigour that they easily defeated the enemy. In this incident the miracles were the throwing of the sand and the huge numbers of non-believers who were killed. The Prophet صلى الله عليه وسلم may have thrown the sand, and the Companions may have killed the enemy, but all these were the acts of Allâh.

Chapter 12

CUSTOM AND *SHIRK*

One of the main reasons for the continuing of *Shirk* practices is custom. Just as nations have their own political, social and national customs, so they have their misguided religious customs. New ideas and practices are formed in the name of religion even though they may be completely opposed to the teachings of that religion.

The Jews and Christians remember and celebrate the births and deaths of their great leaders. Special ceremonies are held, tombs are erected, even special foods are eaten, although there is no evidence whatsoever in the Old and New Testaments for such practices. In fact, the Scriptures oppose such practices as they insist on the Oneness of God. If these people are questioned concerning the validity of their practices, they reply that their families, tribes and countries have done so for centuries and so they are following in the firm footsteps of their ancestors.

The Qur'an ridicules such logic:

﴿ وَإِذَا قِيلَ لَهُمُ ٱتَّبِعُوا۟ مَآ أَنزَلَ ٱللَّهُ قَالُوا۟ بَلْ نَتَّبِعُ مَا وَجَدْنَا عَلَيْهِ ءَابَآءَنَآ ۚ أَوَلَوْ كَانَ ٱلشَّيْطَـٰنُ يَدْعُوهُمْ إِلَىٰ عَذَابِ ٱلسَّعِيرِ ﴾ [لقمان: ٢١]

> "When they are told to follow what Allâh revealed, they say: Nay, we shall follow the ways on which we found our fathers. What! even if it is Satan beckoning them to the penalty of the blazing Fire?" (Luqman: 21)

Islam accepts that love for your country and people is a natural phenomenon, but rejects that this is a valid reason for continuing *Shirk* practices. To follow your ancestors is not compulsory, and neither it is practical at times. Our ancestors included tyrants, blood-thirsty criminals and unjust leaders. Would we, their children, think it a part of our tradition to imitate their actions?

Our ancestors rode on camels and horses, wore the skins of animals, worked on the land and did everything by hand. By inventing and using cars, roads, machines and computers, we have rejected their tradition. No-one has ever disputed all the scientific advances being made around us, but when someone questions the 'religious' practices of forefathers and ancestors, it becomes a very serious issue indeed. The person is punished, not for disputing the tradition, but for disputing the religion itself, even though that particular tradition has no validity in the religion of the people.

The Qur'an also stresses that customs and practices that are introduced into religions are actually the works of Satan. He knows that man is weak and prefers the easy way to the hard way. He deludes people into believing that *Tawheed* is a long and arduous journey of prayers, fasting, self-denial and hardship, the aim of which is to please Allâh, and this aim can very easily be attained by a much shorter and more pleasant route: the route of *Shirk*. He thus uses his influence over ignorant people to introduce a hollow structure of rituals and rites which adopt the name of revealed religion.

The path of *Tawheed* is difficult because it demands that man use his physical and mental abilities to understand Allâh's message, to study it and to practise it. It demands that if man wishes to be successful in front of Allâh, he must discipline his desires, cleanse his soul and obey all Allâh's commands. It is a life-long journey and requires much patience and perseverance.

Satan, on the other hand, rejects the need for such self-control. The path, he offers, is short and sweet. All that man has to do is to seek the patronage of a religious leader, offer sacrifices and gifts to him, build memorials to his name and pray to him. All prayers will be answered and all problems will be resolved. This path is short, entertaining and very attractive.

The elite and *Shirk*

Very often, practices of *Shirk* continue to flourish because they receive the blessings of the rich and elite members of the community. These people use the elaborate rituals and rites to parade their wealth and increase their prestige. Overawed and dazzled, the poor do their best to imitate such splendour, but succeed only in making their own lives even more miserable and wretched.

﴿وَكَذَٰلِكَ مَآ أَرْسَلْنَا مِن قَبْلِكَ فِى قَرْيَةٍ مِّن نَّذِيرٍ إِلَّا قَالَ مُتْرَفُوهَآ إِنَّا وَجَدْنَآ ءَابَآءَنَا عَلَىٰٓ أُمَّةٍ وَإِنَّا عَلَىٰٓ ءَاثَٰرِهِم مُّقْتَدُونَ﴾ [الزخرف: ٢٣]

> "Just in the same way, whenever We sent a warner before you to a people, the wealthy ones among them said: We found our fathers following a certain religion, and we will certainly follow in their footsteps." (Az-Zukhruf: 23)

History has repeatedly shown that it is the privileged classes that are usually behind hypocrisy and falsehood. By encouraging religious extravagance, they not only improve their own positions but also push the poor further and further into debt. This makes the poor completely dependent on the rich and forces them into lives of servitude. If the poor were not shackled by the bonds of expensive ceremonies and customs, they would be in a better position to achieve economic independence and to demand equal rights. It is thus in the interest of the rich to increase the gap between the rich and the poor, and they succeed in this by inventing more and more rites in the name of religion.

The Pharisees

Shirk often spreads because of the ignorance and negligence of its religious scholars. A quick glance at the Bible shows that the responsibility for the death of *Tawheed* and the birth of *Shirk* among the Jews and the Christians lay at the hands of their rabbis and priests. These men apparently led very disciplined, devotional and mystical lives, but were in reality irreligious, selfish and greedy. Their religious garb was simply a tool for deceiving people and collecting as much wealth as they could.

In Matthew ch. 23, we hear Jesus addressing the Rabbis:

> "Everything they do is done for men to see … they love the place of honour at banquets and the most important seats in the synagogues; they love to be greeted in the market-places and to have men call them 'Rabbi' … you hypocrites! You devour widows' houses and for a show make lengthy prayers. Therefore you will be punished more severely.
>
> … Woe to you, teachers of the law and Pharisees, you hypocrites! You shut the kingdom of heaven in men's faces. You yourselves do not enter, nor will you let those enter who are trying to … You travel over land and sea to win a single convert, and when he becomes one, you make him twice as much a son of Hell as you are …
>
> Woe to you … You are like white-washed tombs, which look beautiful on the outside but on the inside are full of dead men's bones and everything unclean. In the same way, on the outside you appear to people as righteous but on the inside you are full of hypocrisy and wickedness.
>
> Woe to you … You build tombs for the Prophets and decorate the graves of the righteous." (Matthew ch. 23)

It is thus very clear that the Jewish scholars wanted fame and fortune at the expense of faith and salvation. Their greed was such that even a poor widow's few possessions were at risk. In order to ensure that people would continue to come to them, they preached that divine favour could not be attained without their advice. They paid homage to their Prophets in order to line their own pockets.

The Qur'an has also exposed the true nature of such charlatans:

﴿ ۞ يَٰٓأَيُّهَا ٱلَّذِينَ ءَامَنُوٓاْ إِنَّ كَثِيرًا مِّنَ ٱلۡأَحۡبَارِ وَٱلرُّهۡبَانِ لَيَأۡكُلُونَ أَمۡوَٰلَ ٱلنَّاسِ بِٱلۡبَٰطِلِ وَيَصُدُّونَ عَن سَبِيلِ ٱللَّهِۗ ﴾ [التوبة : ٣٤]

> "O you who believe! There are indeed many among the rabbis and priests, who in falsehood devour the substance of men and hinder them from the way of Allâh. (At-Taubah: 34)

"Devouring the substance of Men" does not mean that the rabbis and priests have turned into gun-wielding robbers and highwaymen. And neither does "hindering people from the way of Allâh" mean that they actively discourage people from prayer, charity and attending places of worship. What the Qur'an's saying is that these so-called scholars mislead people about their religion by ignoring the teachings of their Prophets and initiating new practices under the guise of religion. The purpose of thus deforming their faith is solely to gather more wealth.

The situation has become so corrupt that neither the crowning of a king nor the funeral of a pauper can take place unless the purses of these parasites have been filled. But the industry of using religion to amass personal fortunes was not to be confined to the Children of Israel. The Prophet Muhammad (صلى الله عليه وسلم) was convinced that similar pharisees would be born among the Muslims. Ibn Maja reports that the Prophet صلى الله عليه وسلم said:

> "There will be people from among my followers who will understand the religion and read the Qur'an, and will say that we go to the notables in order to gain some of the world, but we keep our religion away from them. But this can never happen. Just as you cannot closely approach a thorny tree without being pricked, so you cannot go near them without being affected by their evil."

Today we see that religion as an industry has become a flourishing source of income for unscrupulous saints and self-appointed religious leaders among the Muslims. Tombs are built, offerings are made and prayers are said in order to win their intercession on the Day of Judgment. Every year a fair is organized around their tombs and graves. All conceivable attractions are present to lure people and empty their purses. Games, music and other entertainment for the pleasure seeking; trade and profits for the merchants; gambling facilities and even drugs. For the more pious devotees, story-tellers relate the heroic deeds of their saints, recount their mystical powers and sing their praises. Religion has become a booming business.

And so, although the example given in the Qur'an is that of the Jews, we Muslims today have no excuse for complacency. The situation in the current Muslim world is far worse. The teachings of Allâh and His final Prophet صلى الله عليه وسلم have been abandoned. Worship of the Almighty alone has been replaced by worship of Syyedina Ali, Hussein and Khwaja Mu'eenuddin Chishti. If we Muslims want to escape the curse that Allâh has placed on the Jews for their hypocrisy and ingratitude, it is about time that we followed Allâh's commandments, left *Shirk* and adopted *Tawheed* in its purest form.

Chapter 13

EXCESS AND EXAGGERATION

One of the reasons for the spread of *Shirk* has been excessive reverence for religious leaders. The Qur'an warns:

﴿يَٰٓأَهۡلَ ٱلۡكِتَٰبِ لَا تَغۡلُواْ فِي دِينِكُمۡ﴾ [النساء: ١٧١]

"O people of the Book! Commit no excess in your religion." (An-Nisâ': 171)

But when the Jews and the Christians were praising and remembering their Prophets, they would often forget the path of moderation and adopt the path of exaggeration. Imaginary incidents and fantastic stories would be ascribed to their leaders. Although such excessive praise may have been motivated by extreme love and respect, it was certainly not motivated by a regard for the truth. Religion began to be propagated through the medium of emotive poetry which appealed to the emotions of the listeners rather than to their minds. This led to bigotry, narrow-mindedness, stubbornness and self-delusion. Islam encourages people to see everything in the mirror of reality. To deny something its true worth is wrong, but to exalt it to too high a status is sheer stupidity. The Qur'an has negated many of these exaggerated stories, example of which now follow.

1. Deification of the Prophets

Singers and poets among the Jews and the Christians were very prone to exaggeration. Carried away by praise of the Prophets, they had few qualms about pronouncing them to be sons of the Almighty.

﴿وَقَالَتِ ٱلْيَهُودُ عُزَيْرٌ ٱبْنُ ٱللَّهِ وَقَالَتِ ٱلنَّصَـٰرَى ٱلْمَسِيحُ ٱبْنُ ٱللَّهِ ۖ ذَٰلِكَ قَوْلُهُم بِأَفْوَٰهِهِمْ ۖ يُضَـٰهِـُٔونَ قَوْلَ ٱلَّذِينَ كَفَرُوا۟ مِن قَبْلُ ۚ قَـٰتَلَهُمُ ٱللَّهُ ۚ أَنَّىٰ يُؤْفَكُونَ﴾ [التوبة : ٣٠]

"The Jews say: Uzair is the son of Allâh, and the Christians say: Christ is the son of Allâh. That is a saying from their mouths; in this they imitate what the unbelievers of old used to say. Allâh's curse be on them: how they are deluded away from the truth." (At-Taubah: 30)

Exaggeration is only a step away from lying and when a person lies, he never knows when to stop. The time was not far off when the Christians claimed that Jesus was Allâh Himself, and not merely the son of Allâh.

﴿لَقَدْ كَفَرَ ٱلَّذِينَ قَالُوٓا۟ إِنَّ ٱللَّهَ هُوَ ٱلْمَسِيحُ ٱبْنُ مَرْيَمَ ۖ وَقَالَ ٱلْمَسِيحُ يَـٰبَنِىٓ إِسْرَٰٓءِيلَ ٱعْبُدُوا۟ ٱللَّهَ رَبِّى وَرَبَّكُمْ ۖ إِنَّهُۥ مَن يُشْرِكْ بِٱللَّهِ فَقَدْ حَرَّمَ ٱللَّهُ عَلَيْهِ ٱلْجَنَّةَ وَمَأْوَىٰهُ ٱلنَّارُ ۖ وَمَا لِلظَّـٰلِمِينَ مِنْ أَنصَارٍ﴾ [المائدة : ٧٢]

"They do blaspheme who say: Allâh is Christ the son of Mary. But Christ said: O Children of Israel! Worship Allâh, my Lord and your Lord. Whoever commits *Shirk* with Allâh, Allâh will forbid for him Heaven, and the Fire will be his abode. There will be no help for the wrong-doers." (Al-Maida: 72)

2. Special privileges for special people

The Children of Israel were the descendants of Prophet Yusuf, Ya'qoub, Ishaaq and Ibrahim (عليهم السلام). The presence of so many Prophets in their family tree led to a belief in racial superiority among them. They began to claim that Allâh Almighty has specially favoured them and treated them as his own children.

﴿وَقَالَتِ ٱلْيَهُودُ وَٱلنَّصَـٰرَىٰ نَحْنُ أَبْنَـٰٓؤُا۟ ٱللَّهِ وَأَحِبَّـٰٓؤُهُۥ﴾ [المائدة : ١٨]

"The Jews and the Christians say: We are the sons of Allâh and his beloved ones." (Al-Mâ'ida:18)

The Qur'an rejects such a blasphemous notion:

﴿ وَأَنَّهُۥ تَعَٰلَىٰ جَدُّ رَبِّنَا مَا ٱتَّخَذَ صَٰحِبَةً وَلَا وَلَدًا ﴾ [الجن : ٣]

"And exalted is the Majesty of our Lord: He has taken neither a wife nor a son." (Al-Jinn:3)

But the arrogance of the Jews knew no bounds. They believed that as a race they were superior to the rest of Allâh's creatures, and that Heaven had been guaranteed for them. Their actions in this world were of little consequence, and if one of them committed an unforgivable sin, their Prophets would easily get him pardoned. Even if that person was not forgiven and thrown into Hell, Allâh would never allow him to remain in the fire for more than forty days.

﴿ وَقَالُوا۟ لَن تَمَسَّنَا ٱلنَّارُ إِلَّآ أَيَّامًا مَّعْدُودَةً ۚ قُلْ أَتَّخَذْتُمْ عِندَ ٱللَّهِ عَهْدًا فَلَن يُخْلِفَ ٱللَّهُ عَهْدَهُۥٓ ۖ أَمْ تَقُولُونَ عَلَى ٱللَّهِ مَا لَا تَعْلَمُونَ ﴾ [البقرة : ٨٠]

"And they say: the Fire shall not touch us except for a few numbered days. Say: Have you taken a promise from Allâh as Allâh does not break His promises? Or are you saying about Allâh what you do not know?" (Al-Baqarah:80)

Islam believes in justice for all, and cannot accept that whereas ordinary sinners will be punished, Jewish sinners will be pardoned. If a person from among a noble and good family commits an evil, Allâh does not forgive him because of his family, but instead dissociates him from them. The Qur'an gives the example of Prophet Noah and his unbelieving son.

The disbelief and ingratitude of the Prophet's nation had brought Allâh's punishment and anger on them: their sins had become a raging thunderstorm, they were being swept away by savage floods, and the earth was soon to be cleansed of their impure presence. At this critical time the noble Prophet صلى الله عليه وسلم pleaded to Allâh:

﴿ وَنَادَىٰ نُوحٌ رَّبَّهُۥ فَقَالَ رَبِّ إِنَّ ٱبْنِى مِنْ أَهْلِى وَإِنَّ وَعْدَكَ ٱلْحَقُّ وَأَنتَ أَحْكَمُ ٱلْحَٰكِمِينَ ﴾ [هود: ٤٥]

"O my Lord! Surely my son is of my family! And Your promise is true, and You are the most Just of all judges." (Hud:45)

But Allâh Almighty could not accept this plea:

﴿ قَالَ يَٰنُوحُ إِنَّهُۥ لَيْسَ مِنْ أَهْلِكَ ۖ إِنَّهُۥ عَمَلٌ غَيْرُ صَٰلِحٍ ۖ فَلَا تَسْـَٔلْنِ مَا لَيْسَ لَكَ بِهِۦ عِلْمٌ ۖ إِنِّىٓ أَعِظُكَ أَن تَكُونَ مِنَ ٱلْجَٰهِلِينَ ﴾ [هود: ٤٦]

"He said: O Noah! He is not of your family: his conduct is unrighteous. So do not ask me that of which you have no knowledge. I advise you, lest you act like the ignorant." (Hud: 46)

3. Religious scholars can say no wrong

Nations through the ages have been the slaves of their kings and the devotees of their scholars. They have accepted the words of their kings as law, and the rulings of their religious scholars as divine.

﴿ ٱتَّخَذُوٓا۟ أَحْبَارَهُمْ وَرُهْبَٰنَهُمْ أَرْبَابًا مِّن دُونِ ٱللَّهِ وَٱلْمَسِيحَ ٱبْنَ مَرْيَمَ وَمَآ أُمِرُوٓا۟ إِلَّا لِيَعْبُدُوٓا۟ إِلَٰهًا وَٰحِدًا ۖ لَّآ إِلَٰهَ إِلَّا هُوَ ۚ سُبْحَٰنَهُۥ عَمَّا يُشْرِكُونَ ﴾ [التوبة: ٣١]

"They take their priests and their rabbis to be their lords instead of Allâh. And they also take Christ the son of Mary. Yet they were commanded only to worship One Lord. There is no god but He. Praise and Glory to Him. Far He is from those who commit *Shirk*." (At-Taubah: 31)

At the time that the above verse was revealed, Adi bin Hatim (رضي الله عنه) had renounced Christianity and embraced Islam. He was a scholar of Christianity, and told the Prophet صلى الله عليه وسلم that no Christian worships his priest.

The Prophet صلى الله عليه وسلم replied:

> "It is true that they do not worship them. But when they (the priests) legitimize something, they (the Christians) accept it as legitimate. And when they forbid something, they accept it as forbidden. And that is the same as worshipping them."

Such blind obedience of religious men is common among Muslims today. They will accept some of the most judicious rules, without thinking and without looking for evidence in the Qur'an and Sunnah.

4. The Prophet صلى الله عليه وسلم cannot alter divine revelation

During the time of Prophet Muhammad (صلى الله عليه وسلم), when the fight between Truth and Injustice was at its height, the *Mushrik* Arabs asked the Prophet صلى الله عليه وسلم to change some of the uncompromising verses contained in the Qur'an. They said that they were willing to agree to peace if the contents of the Qur'an were slightly modified to suit them. The following verse was revealed in response to their request.

﴿وَإِذَا تُتْلَىٰ عَلَيْهِمْ ءَايَاتُنَا بَيِّنَٰتٍ قَالَ ٱلَّذِينَ لَا يَرْجُونَ لِقَآءَنَا ٱئْتِ بِقُرْءَانٍ غَيْرِ هَٰذَآ أَوْ بَدِّلْهُ قُلْ مَا يَكُونُ لِىٓ أَنْ أُبَدِّلَهُۥ مِن تِلْقَآئِ نَفْسِىٓ إِنْ أَتَّبِعُ إِلَّا مَا يُوحَىٰٓ إِلَىَّ إِنِّىٓ أَخَافُ إِنْ عَصَيْتُ رَبِّى عَذَابَ يَوْمٍ عَظِيمٍ﴾

[يونس : ١٥]

"But when Our clear signs are recited to them, those who do not rest their hope on their meeting with Us, say: Bring us a Reading other than this, or change this. Say: it is not for me of my own accord to change it: I follow naught but what is revealed unto me. If I were to disobey my Lord, I would fear the penalty of Great Day." (Yunus: 15)

It is thus very clear that the Prophet صلى الله عليه وسلم could of his own accord make no alterations in the divine message. He had to transmit the verses to his people exactly as they were revealed to him. If the great Prophet Muhammad (صلى الله عليه وسلم), the perfect and enduring example to all mankind, could not change or modify the divine law, how then can we accept that the scholars and saints who came centuries after him, could have any hope of changing it. The Prophet صلى الله عليه وسلم was not allowed to add tenets to the faith of Allâh, so who has given today's scholars the authority to do so?

Islam has not forbidden us to honour and respect our elders and learned men. In fact, it has emphasized this quality in a Muslim. But this does not give the scholars *carte blanche* to play havoc with Allâh's religion. Their work should be confined to practising the commandments contained in the Qur'an and Sunnah and to inviting others to do the same, not to inventing their own version of Islam. The person who gives the teachings of such scholars the status of religion is a *Mushrik*.

﴿ أَمْ لَهُمْ شُرَكَـٰٓؤُا۟ شَرَعُوا۟ لَهُم مِّنَ ٱلدِّينِ مَا لَمْ يَأْذَنۢ بِهِ ٱللَّهُ ۚ وَلَوْلَا كَلِمَةُ ٱلْفَصْلِ لَقُضِىَ بَيْنَهُمْ ۗ وَإِنَّ ٱلظَّـٰلِمِينَ لَهُمْ عَذَابٌ أَلِيمٌ ﴾

[الشورى: ٢١]

"What! Do they have partners (in godliness) who have established for them some religion without the permission of Allâh? Had it not been for the Decree of Judgment, the matter between them would have been decided at once. And indeed the wrong-doers will have a grievous punishment." (Ash-Shura: 21)

The "partners" referred to in the above verse are the religious scholars who sell charms and prayers of their own manufacture. Their trade is one of competitions with the true teachings of Islam. Muslims should always remember that it is the prerogative of Allâh Almighty to pronounce something as being part of faith, to judge whether something is *Halaal* or *Haraam*, to announce whether a particular action will lead to punishment or reward. He alone has the right to determine such things, and He alone has the right to tell mankind of His decision through His chosen Prophets. No human being has the right to interfere or to change the decision of Allâh, least of all the bogus scholars who have made religion a very profitable business.

5. Walis (saints) are not better than Prophets

Among the Sufis we find the belief that some saints are more important than the Messengers and Prophets of Allâh. These saints are supposed to have more knowledge than the Prophets and are closer to Allâh. The consequence of such a belief is that these saints do not need to follow the message preached by the Prophets and so all that has been forbidden in divine religion is *Halaal* for them. The Sufis describe Ibn Al-Arabi as the greatest scholar, and one of his most famous verses is that:

مَقَامُ النُّبُوَّةِ فِي بَرْزَخ   فُوَيْقَ الرَّسُولِ دُونَ الْوَلّى

> "The position of a Prophet is at a gap (Barzakh). He is above the Messenger and below the Wali."

Such a belief requires Muslims to follow saints rather than Prophets as they profess to have a higher status. Needless to say, it is an ignorant and false belief that has no evidence in the Book of Allâh.

6. Deserting the tenets of Islam

One of the groups that claim to be Muslims are the Batinies who have rejected some of the fundamentals of Islam such as prayer, fasting, Zakat and Hajj. Their argument is that the Prophet (صلى الله عليه وسلم), the Companions and the entire Muslim Ummah have misinterpreted the requirements that Allâh has laid down in the Qur'an. They thus claim to have an even better understanding of the Book of Allâh than the Prophet صلى الله عليه وسلم who received it by divine inspiration.

This chapter has discussed the liberties that were taken with the character and the message of the Prophet صلى الله عليه وسلم by various groups. The Prophet (صلى الله عليه وسلم) was himself aware of this danger and warned his followers to stay clear of it.

لا تطرونى كما اطرت النصارى ابن مريم فإنما أنا عبد فقولوا عبدالله ورسوله (رواه البخارى)

"Do not praise me excessively as the Christians praise Christ, son of Mary, for I am the servant of Allâh and His Prophet." (Bukhâri)

Chapter 14

GOD INCARNATE

This is the theory that when mankind is in serious trouble, Allâh comes to their rescue by adopting the form of a human being and leading the people out of their situation. The Arabic word for this concept is "*Hulool*". It has been part of the faith of many of the world's religions. The Hindus believe that God split himself into various deities, all of which came down to earth in human or animal forms. The Buddhists believe that the Buddha was a divine figure, and the Parsis have a similar belief about Zoroaster. The Jews believe that Prophets Dawud, Yaqoub and Uzair (عليهم السلام) were the sons of Allâh, with divine characteristics and a mission to help the Children of Israel. But the concept of *Hulool* is best embodied in the Christian Trinity. God was able to divide himself into three different forms, all of which were separate yet part of the divine whole.

Unfortunately, the concept of *Hulool* entered into Islam very early. Its first propagator was Abdullah Ibn Saba who lived during the reign of the Caliph Umar (رضي الله عنه). Ibn Saba claimed that Allâh had become incarnate in the person of the Prophet's cousin Ali. By the time Ali became Caliph, the number of people who accepted Ibn Saba's claims had increased to seventy. Ali (رضي الله عنه) repeatedly denied that he was Allâh, but the men were adamant in their faith. Finally, the Caliph had these people thrown into fire. But the faith of these *Mushriks* was so strong that even while burning in the flames, they continued to shout "Ali is god". Their punishment had only strengthened their belief because, as far as they were concerned,

"Only the lord of fire can punish with fire."

Hussein Ibn Mansoor Hallaj

Hussein Ibn Mansoor was born in Iran in the second century after the Hijrah. Not only did he preach that the divine can become incarnate in the mortal, but he also claimed that Allâh had taken over his body. He raised the banner of "I am the truth" as a result of which the Abbasid Caliph had him executed in Baghdad in 310 A.H.

A verse that Hallaj used to recite was,

كفرت بدين الله والكفر واجب لدي وعند المسلمين قبيح

"I disobeyed the religion of Allâh. Disobedience is repulsive to the Muslims but it is compulsory for me."

With such pride did this man announce his denial of the faith of Allâh.

The concept of *Hulool* is false

It is absurd to think that Allâh the Almighty feels the need to come down to earth disguised as a man when He wishes to help His creatures. As Master, Creator and Ruler of the universe, He only has to say "Be — and it is!" He has no need to come and live the life of a mortal, suffering his trials, preaching to those who will listen, being ill-treated by the creatures He Himself has created. Can we accept a fate of misery, tears and failure for Him who commands the rains, the winds, the angels, the jinns and the volcanoes? Such a notion is an affront to logic and reason, and is an insult to the Power and Majesty of our Lord.

If we study the lives of those reputed to have been god in disguise, we see very clearly that there was nothing divine about them. These men needed food, water, clothes, shelter and sleep, just as all ordinary mortals do. Their missions met with success, but also with failure and humiliation. And most of all, when their time in this world had ended, they were not able to resist death.

The death of God?

Hindus claim that Krishna was divine, and they also claim that he had to helplessly watch his kingdom being robbed and plundered. The grief at being unable to save his people took him to his death in the snow of the Himalayas. Was the man, who grieved at the suffering of his people, an ordinary mortal or a powerful god?

Buddhists believe that the dead body of the Budddha was cremated in Nepal and that his ashes were buried in eight separate sites, above each of which a memorial was erected. Can such a disfigured and mutilated body be worth the honour of being worshipped?

Christians say that Christ was dragged through Jerusalem carrying a heavy cross, that a crown of thorns was placed on his head, and that he was crucified and then buried. While on the cross, he wept and prayed to his Lord for help. How can we believe that God so helpless that he has to endure such pain and suffering?

Some Muslims invoke the name of Ali (رضي الله عنه) and Hussein (رضي الله عنه) in times of distress. They forget that both Ali and his son were human beings who lived as mortals and died as martyrs. Had they been divine, they would easily have been able to save and defend themselves from their attackers.

Chapter 15

MAN AND GOD ARE ONE?

The concept of *Wahdatul Wujud* ("Unity of Being") has been a major factor in the spread of *Shirk* among the Hindus and the dervishes. The theory supposes that everything on earth is part of God, and that God and His creation are inseparable. The believer, the atheist and the hypocrite, the just and the evil, the camel and the pig, all are one. In form they may look different, but in reality they are all the same.

This concept was introduced into the Muslim world by the Sufi scholar Ibn Al Arabi. In one of his couplets he says: "Dog and pig are nothing but our gods. And whatever is worshipped in the chapel is our god." This is a false and ignorant concept, and contradicts all the teachings of Islam. For example, the Qur'an says that Allâh is Alone and Unique, but this theory claims that Allâh and His creation are all equal. The Qur'an says that Allâh has no parents or children, but the theory claims that all parents and children are Allâh. The Qur'an stresses that Prophet Muhammad (صلى الله عليه وسلم) was the Allâh's Messenger and the ideal example for all of mankind. The concept of *Wahdatul Wujud* does away with the need for following his example as it claims that ordinary people are just as divine and important as the Prophets. It is thus a nihilistic theory which opposes the very foundations of Islam.

Chapter 16

WHY DOESN'T ALLÂH STOP *SHIRK*?

Some people complain that Allâh should put a stop to the numerous practices of *Shirk* if He dislikes them so much.

﴿سَيَقُولُ ٱلَّذِينَ أَشْرَكُوا۟ لَوْ شَآءَ ٱللَّهُ مَآ أَشْرَكْنَا وَلَآ ءَابَآؤُنَا وَلَا حَرَّمْنَا مِن شَىْءٍ﴾ [الأنعام: ١٤٨]

"Those who commit *Shirk* say: If Allâh had wished, neither we nor our fathers would have committed *Shirk*. And neither would we have pronounced things to be *Haraam* that He has not ordered." (Al-An'am: 148)

To answer this complaint, we must understand the nature of our lives. The Qur'an tells us very clearly that our lives are a trial to test our faith. Allâh tests us with wealth, honour and happiness, and with poverty, bondage and disgrace. The person who is successful in these trials is the one who is grateful in times of happiness, and patient in times of difficulty.

﴿فَأَمَّا ٱلْإِنسَٰنُ إِذَا مَا ٱبْتَلَىٰهُ رَبُّهُۥ فَأَكْرَمَهُۥ وَنَعَّمَهُۥ فَيَقُولُ رَبِّىٓ أَكْرَمَنِ ۝ وَأَمَّآ إِذَا مَا ٱبْتَلَىٰهُ فَقَدَرَ عَلَيْهِ رِزْقَهُۥ فَيَقُولُ رَبِّىٓ أَهَٰنَنِ﴾ [الفجر: ١٥-١٦]

"As for man, when his Lord tries him, giving him honour and gifts, then he says, 'My Lord has honoured me." And when He tries him, restricting his subsistence for him, then he says, 'My Lord has humiliated me!" (Al-Fajr: 15,16)

The trial is not a short one but begins at birth and ends only at death. For this reason, we are not necessarily punished or rewarded immediately for our acts. The criminal is not struck down as soon as he kills. The pious and patient worshipper is not immediately rewarded with gold from the sky. And although

Allâh deals justly with the believers and the non-believers, complete divine justice will be awarded on the Day of Judgment. That is when mankind will experience the joy of the gardens of Paradise or the horror of Hell. Practices like those of *Shirk* illustrate the great difference between practices that Allâh likes and those He allows. Allâh does not like *Shirk*, but He allows it to continue in order to test the faith of His subjects. The successful believer is the one who refuses to take the easy path that *Shirk* offers, and instead follows the long and difficult path of *Tawheed.*

It is worth remembering that wealth and fame in this world are not necessarily a sign of Allâh's pleasure, and neither is poverty necessarily a sign of His anger. They are both times of trial in which Allâh tests our gratitude and patience.

﴿ وَمِنَ ٱلنَّاسِ مَن يَعْبُدُ ٱللَّهَ عَلَىٰ حَرْفٍ فَإِنْ أَصَابَهُۥ خَيْرٌ ٱطْمَأَنَّ بِهِۦ وَإِنْ أَصَابَتْهُ فِتْنَةٌ ٱنقَلَبَ عَلَىٰ وَجْهِهِۦ خَسِرَ ٱلدُّنْيَا وَٱلْـَٔاخِرَةَ ذَٰلِكَ هُوَ ٱلْخُسْرَانُ ٱلْمُبِينُ ﴾

[الحج : ١١]

> "There are among people those who worship Allâh on the verge: if good befalls them, they are content with it. And if a trial comes to them, they turn on their faces. They lose both this world and the Hereafter: that is loss for all to see." (Al-Hajj: 11)

"And fight them until oppression is no more."

The blind imitation of custom and tradition has made society blind to injustice and deaf to the screams of the oppressed. Few have dared to oppose the enduring strength of custom. It is thus the duty of the fearless and the just to cleanse the world from injustice and cruelty.

Despite their valour and courage, the Hindu rajahs were unable to rid their country of the dreadful custom of Sati, in which a husband. It was only the rule of Islam that officially banned such a horrific custom for centuries, even using force when necessary.

The early Egyptians believed that when the Nile god was angry, he dried the River Nile and brought drought to the country. The god could only be appeased by the sacrifice of a young and beautiful girl, and so every year the Egyptians held a macabre ceremony in which a young girl was thrown into the river to drown. The people would stand on the river bank to watch the chosen victim struggling desperately against the waves. When Amr bin Aas (رضي الله عنه) conquered Egypt during the reign of the great Muslim Caliph, Umar bin Khattab رضي الله عنه, he used the might of the Muslim armies to permanently stop this horrific celebration which had been called "The Wedding of the Nile."

History shows that all societies have thus practised tyranny and cruelty, whether in the name of progress or in the name of religion. It is the task of the Muslims to obliterate all unjust and oppressive practices and to establish the faith of Allâh on earth.